SandCastle™

Baby Mammals

It's a Baby Mustang!

Kelly Doudna

Consulting Editor, Diane Craig, M.A./Reading Specialist

ABDO
Publishing Company

Published by ABDO Publishing Company, 8000 West 78th Street, Edina, Minnesota 55439.

Printed in the United States.

Editor: Pam Price
Content Developer: Nancy Tuminelly
Cover and Interior Design and Production: Mighty Media
Photo Credits: Digital Vision, Peter Arnold Inc. (J.L. Klein & M.L. Hubert)

Library of Congress Cataloging-in-Publication Data

Doudna, Kelly, 1963-
  It's a baby mustang! / Kelly Doudna.
    p. cm. -- (Baby mammals)
  ISBN 978-1-60453-027-8
1. Mustang--Juvenile literature. 2. Foals--Juvenile literature. I. Title.

SF293.M9D68 2008
636.1'3--dc22

                        2007036930

SandCastle™ Level: Fluent

SandCastle™ books are created by a team of professional educators, reading specialists, and content developers around five essential components—phonemic awareness, phonics, vocabulary, text comprehension, and fluency—to assist young readers as they develop reading skills and strategies and increase their general knowledge. All books are written, reviewed, and leveled for guided reading, early reading intervention, and Accelerated Reader® programs for use in shared, guided, and independent reading and writing activities to support a balanced approach to literacy instruction. The SandCastle™ series has four levels that correspond to early literacy development. The levels are provided to help teachers and parents select appropriate books for young readers.

Emerging Readers
(no flags)

Beginning Readers
(1 flag)

Transitional Readers
(2 flags)

Fluent Readers
(3 flags)

SandCastle™ would like to hear from you. Please send us your comments and suggestions.
sandcastle@abdopublishing.com

Vital Statistics

for the Mustang

BABY NAME
foal

NUMBER IN LITTER
1 or 2, average 1

WEIGHT AT BIRTH
90 pounds

AGE OF INDEPENDENCE
2 years

ADULT WEIGHT
about 1,000 pounds

LIFE EXPECTANCY
20 to 25 years

Mustangs are horses that live in the wild. A baby mustang is called a foal. A mother mustang is a mare.

A father mustang is called
a stallion. A stallion leads
a herd of mares. He fights
other stallions to defend
his herd.

Foals are able to stand and walk two hours after they are born.

At birth, a foal's legs are almost as long as they will ever be.

Like all female mammals, mares produce milk to nurse their babies.

Mustangs are herbivores. They eat grass, sagebrush, juniper, and other scrubby plants.

A mustang's diet is not as nutritious as a domestic horse's.

Mustangs neigh and nicker to communicate with each other. They snort loudly if there is danger.

Wolves and coyotes are the main predators of mustangs. The lead mare takes the herd to safety while the stallion fights the predator.

Adult mustangs form a circle around the foals to protect them.

Foals stay with the herd until they are about two years old. The females are known as fillies. The males are called colts.

Colts leave their birth herds and roam together for a few years. When they are about six years old, they begin to gather their own herds.

Fun Fact

About the Mustang

A mustang foal weighs 90 pounds when it's born. That's about the same weight as a 12-year-old kid.

Glossary

communicate – to share ideas, information, or feelings.

defend – to protect from harm or attack.

domestic – living with or near humans.

expectancy – an expected or likely amount.

herbivore – an animal that eats mainly plants.

herd – a group of animals that are all one kind.

independence – the state of no longer needing others to care for or support you.

nicker – to neigh softly.

nutritious – containing food substances that help living things grow, such as vitamins, minerals, and proteins.

nurse – to feed a baby milk from the breast.

predator – an animal that hunts others.

produce – to make or create something.

To see a complete list of SandCastle™ books and other nonfiction titles from ABDO Publishing Company, visit **www.abdopublishing.com**.

8000 West 78th Street, Edina, MN 55439

800-800-1312 • 952-831-1632 fax